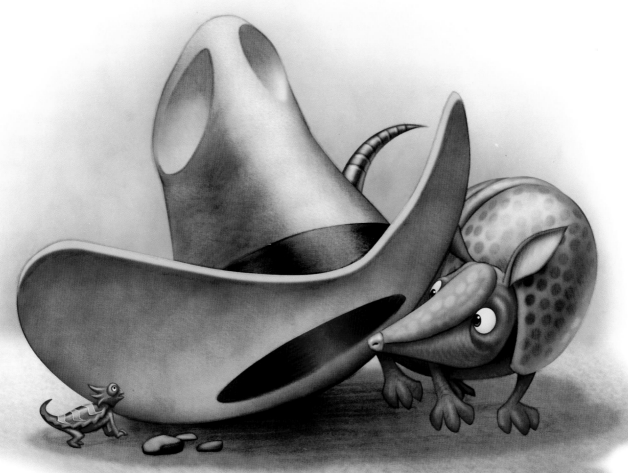

PECOS BILL Invents the Ten-Gallon HAT

By Kevin Strauss

Illustrated by David Harrington

PELICAN PUBLISHING COMPANY

Gretna 2012

For my adventurous girls, Andrea, Sarah, and Annie—K. S.

For my wonderful children, Chase, Nick, and Emma—D. H.

The word "Pelican" and the depiction of a pelican are trademarks of Pelican Publishing Company, Inc., and are registered in the U.S. Patent and Trademark Office.

ISBN 9781455615025
E-book ISBN 9781455615032

The Origin of This Story

While there are many stories about Pecos Bill inventing things such as the lasso, I created this story to explain something else that Pecos Bill probably invented. For more traditional and original stories about Pecos Bill, search "Pecos Bill" in your library catalog or online.

Printed in Singapore
Published by Pelican Publishing Company, Inc.
1000 Burmaster Street, Gretna, Louisiana 70053

Pecos Bill Invents the Ten-Gallon Hat

Before Pecos Bill, cowboys didn't know how to do much of anything. They didn't know how to rope cattle. They didn't know how to drive cattle. And they had no idea how to deal with the hot Texas sun.

One day, Pecos Bill was working a herd near the Rio Grande, and the sun was hot enough to fry bacon on a boulder. Looking around, he saw that it was nice and shady under the cottonwood trees by the river, so he rode over to cool off under one.

It was comfortable there, but that wasn't where the cattle were. "That's okay," thought Bill. "If the cattle want to stay on the prairie, I got a mind to move the tree."

He tied his rattlesnake rope around the biggest cottonwood on the river and said *giddyup* to his horse. Now, no ordinary horse could move a tree like that, but Bill didn't have an ordinary horse. He had Lightning, a horse that packed more wallop than a prairie thunderstorm. The black stallion pulled and pulled, and the roots—*pop!*—jumped right out of the ground. But the tree fell—*fwump*—burying twenty head of cattle in branches and leaves.

Pecos Bill had to spend the rest of that day digging those cows out.

But Bill wasn't one to give up after just one try.

"Well, if I can't move the whole dang tree, maybe I can move the shady part," he thought.

For a while it worked fine.
The trouble started when Bill got to
town and tried to walk into a hotel.
He opened the door and—*bam!*—fell
right on his rear end.

Pecos Bill got up and ran at the
door again, but—*bam!*—he landed
flat on his back. Then he realized
why he didn't fit through the door.

But Pecos wasn't one to be flummoxed
after just two tries. The next day, he
went walking through town. It was a
Saturday, and when he got to the end
of the main street, he saw a group of
men playing some sort of newfangled
ballgame.

But it wasn't the men's game that interested
Pecos Bill. It was their caps. It looked as if
those caps kept the sun off the players' faces.

Bill bought a cap at the store, and the next day, he wore it out on the prairie. The cap kept the sun off his face all right, but that sky fire still burned the back of his neck. Then when a thunderstorm came up, the rain soaked the cloth cap.

"Well, that didn't pan out," thought
Pecos Bill.
    Not one to cash it in after only three
tries, Pecos Bill went to town the next
day looking for another hat. As he was
walking down the main street, he heard a
clanging bell. Bill dove out of the way as
a horse-drawn fire wagon rushed past him.

As he lay there in the dust, Bill could see smoke coming from the livery stable.

Pecos Bill whistled up Lightning and rode out of town lickety-split. He pulled out his rattlesnake rope, lassoed up a storm cloud, and dragged it back to town. He hogtied the cloud and squeezed it so hard that it gushed rain, dowsing the flames.

The volunteer firefighters were so happy
that they made Pecos Bill an honorary
member of the fire brigade and gave him
his very own metal firefighter helmet.
"I reckon this might be just what I need,"
said Bill.

While the back brim of the helmet shaded his neck, the metal got hotter and hotter in the sun. By noon, Pecos Bill took off the helmet and wrapped a wet bandanna around his head.

Not one to skedaddle after only four tries, Pecos Bill sat on his bedroll that night figuring about hats.

"The baseball cap only shaded my face, and it didn't keep me dry. The firefighter helmet shaded my neck, but it got too hot. . . . "

Just then, Lightning bent down and pushed the two hats together. That gave Bill an idea.
"Wait a minute! What if I made a hat with a wide brim, like a baseball cap, to shade my neck, and a high crown, like a firefighter helmet, to shed the rain, and in a waterproof fabric, so it wouldn't get too hot?"

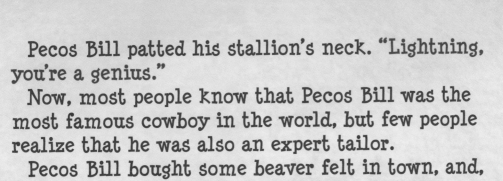

Pecos Bill patted his stallion's neck. "Lightning, you're a genius."

Now, most people know that Pecos Bill was the most famous cowboy in the world, but few people realize that he was also an expert tailor.

Pecos Bill bought some beaver felt in town, and, using his baseball cap and firefighter helmet as models, he sewed and pressed the very first ten-gallon hat.

After that, Pecos Bill would carry his own shade wherever he went. And when it rained, the water just rolled right off the crown and over the brim, leaving Pecos Bill's head nice and dry. What's more, it made a handy bowl.

When other cowboys saw how useful Pecos Bill's invention was, they gave a big *yeehaw* and ordered some of their own. Pretty soon, even the brand-new greenhorn cowboys were wearing them.

I'm telling you, that's the way it was, that's the way it is, and that's the end of the story.

Cowboy Gear

Everything that a cowboy wears has an important purpose.

Cowboy Hat

A cowboy hat gives a cowboy shade on the treeless prairie. Rain drains off the front and back of the hat, keeping a cowboy dry. He can also use it like a bowl to give water to his horse or as a washbasin out on the prairie.

Bandanna

Cowboys pull bandannas over their mouths during dust storms or when they are riding behind cattle that are kicking up dirt.

Chaps

Thick leather chaps protect a cowboy's legs from thorn bushes and sharp cow horns as he rides in the prairie and chaparral.

Cowboy Boots

Cowboy boots are high to keep pebbles out. They have pointed toes and tall heels to help them fit into the horse's saddle stirrups.